THE FACE

A TIME CODE

RUTH OZEKI

THE FACE

A TIME CODE

RESTLESS BOOKS
BROOKLYN, NEW YORK

Digital edition published by Restless Books, 2015
This edition published by Restless Books, 2016

Cover design by Kristen Radtke
Set in Garibaldi by Tetragon, London

Library of Congress Cataloging-in-Publication
Data: Available upon request.

ISBN: 978-1-63206-0-525

Printed in the United States of America

Ellison, Stavans, and Hochstein LP
232 3rd Street, Suite A111
Brooklyn, NY 11215
www.restlessbooks.com
publisher@restlessbooks.com

PROLOGUE: A KOAN

What did your face look like before your parents were born?

I first read this koan when I was eight or maybe nine years old. Someone had given me a little book called *Zen Buddhism*—or perhaps the book had belonged to my parents and I'd taken it from their shelves, thinking it ought to be mine. The book was small and slim, the perfect size for a child to hold, but more importantly, it had a friendly face, which made it stand out from the other duller books on my parents' shelves. A book's face is its cover, and this one, with its simple flowers against a muted orange background, appealed to me. A solid black box in the upper right corner contained the title: ZEN. The letters were tall and hand-drawn, in a floaty, white, Art Nouveau font that looked like ghosts, dancing. Beneath, in very small caps, was the word BUDDHISM.

Inside the cover was the subtitle: *An Introduction to Zen with Stories, Parables and Koan Riddles of the Zen Masters, decorated with figures from old Chinese ink-paintings*—an exceedingly long subtitle for such a small book. It was published in 1959 by Peter Pauper Press, and I know this because I did an online image search for "Zen Buddhism small orange book," and there it was, a familiar face, instantly recognizable, looking out at me from my computer screen after more than five decades.

The little book was a talisman, a teacher, a gate. It was filled with gnomic tales of old Zen masters posing paradoxical questions that confounded my nine-year-old notions of rational narrative in a way I found both fascinating and perplexing, and so I assumed they must be profound and very wise.

> *What is the sound of one hand clapping?*
> *How can one catch hold of Emptiness?*
> *Does a dog have buddha nature?*
> *When there is neither "I" nor "you," who is it*
> *who seeks the Way?*

Listed like this, these koans might sound clichéd, but they were brand new to me. The crazy old Zen masters, with their staffs and whisks and comic antics, who were always slapping and cuffing each other, cutting off their arms and eyelids, and pulling each other's ears and noses, seemed to hold a key to my nine-year-old identity.

What is your original face?

I read the koans earnestly, searching for an answer.

TIME CODE 00:00:00

00:00:00   I've put the mirror on the altar where the Buddha used to be. Laptop's just below it. Fussing now with the seating, arranging the cushions. How close should I be? How much proximity can I tolerate? How is the lighting? Flattering? Unflattering? Does it matter? Should I change into a turtleneck to hide the lines on my neck? Hide them from whom? Is the neck even part of the face, and do I need to wash my hair? Do I need reading glasses, or can I type without them? Can I *see* without them? No, no glasses. No need to look at the computer screen. Just face and me, facing off in the mirror.

00:04:14 Okay. Ready. No, wait, there's dust on the mirror. Must clean it. Do I have vinegar? Yes, under the sink.

00:07:26 Mirror's spotless.

00:08:56 How do I start?

THE EXPERIMENT

The experiment is simple: to sit in front of a mirror and watch my face for three hours. It's a variation of an observation experiment I came across in "The Power of Patience,"* an essay about the pedagogical benefits of immersive attention by Jennifer L. Roberts, a professor of art history and architecture at Harvard. In her essay, Professor Roberts describes an assignment she gives her students each year: to go to a museum or gallery and spend three full hours observing a single work of art and making a detailed record

---

* Jennifer L. Roberts, "The Power of Patience," *Harvard Magazine* (November-December, 2013).

of the observations, questions, and speculations that arise over that time. The three-hour assignment, she admits, is designed to feel excessively long. "Painfully" is the word she uses, asserting that anything less painful will not yield the benefits of the immersive attention that she seeks to teach. Paintings are "time batteries," she writes, quoting art historian David Joselit. They are "exorbitant stockpiles" of temporal experience and information that can only be tapped and unpacked using the skills of slow processing and strategic patience—skills that our impatient world has caused to atrophy. She's trying to help her students develop their stunted skill set so they will learn not simply to look at art, but to *see* it.

My face is not a work of art. There is no reason for me to look at it other than to make sure there's no spinach stuck between my teeth. I rarely put on makeup. My hair seems to take care of itself, more or less. But after reading Roberts's article, it occurred to me that a face is a time battery, too, a stockpile of experience, and I began to wonder what my fifty-nine-year-old face might reveal if I could bear to look at it for three hours—a painfully long time, indeed.

My relationship with my reflection has changed over the years. As a young child, I was indifferent to my reflected self. As I grew a bit older, I turned shy and avoided my reflection, but by the time I was a teenager, I was spending lavish amounts of time in front of mirrors, scrutinizing every follicle and pore, and developing a minute and almost microscopic relationship with my surfaces. I don't think I was different from most American teenagers in this way. The compulsive self-regard continued into the early years of my adulthood and then diminished as I aged. Now, although I still check my reflection in shop windows and glance at my face when I'm washing my hands or brushing my teeth, I spend very little time in front of mirrors. And yet, over a lifetime it adds up to... what? Hundreds of hours? Days or weeks or months even?

Three more hours should be doable, but I'm loath to start. Why? Is it vanity? Anti-vanity? How would I know? What does fifty-nine-year-old vanity look like, anyway? Fifty-nine is a difficult age for a face. Menopause wreaks havoc with a face's sense of self, and the changes are rapid and cascading. It's like puberty in reverse. At fifty-nine, I never quite know what my face will be when I wake up in the morning.

Mirror, mirror on the wall, who's the fairest of them all? mutters the aging queen.

Our tales all tell us that an old woman's vanity is, at best, sad and unseemly, and, at worst, ridiculous or even evil. As I approach my sixtieth year, I feel I should be moving away from the question *Am I still fair?* toward a more existential question: *Am I still here?* You'd think seeing myself in a mirror would be somewhat reassuring.

And yet, recently I've noticed that when I catch sight of my face in a shop window, I'm quick to look away. When I brush my teeth, I'll often turn my back to the mirror, or focus on a detail of my reflection, a blemish or a spot, rather than on my aspect as a whole. It's not that I don't like what I see, although that's often part of it. Rather, it's more that I don't quite *recognize* myself in my reflection anymore, and so I'm always startled. Averting my gaze is a reflexive reaction, a kind of uncanny valley response to the sight of this person who is no longer quite me.

It's not polite to stare at strangers.

*

In Zen teachings, *impermanence* is the first of the three marks of existence. Everything changes, nothing stays the same. The second mark of existence is *no-self*, which derives from the first: if everything changes and nothing stays the same, then there is no such thing as a fixed self. The self is only a passing notion, a changing story, relative to its momentary position in space and time. *Suffering*, the third mark of existence, derives quite logically from the first two. We don't like impermanence, we want to *be* someone, a fixed self, and we want that self to last. Lacking that fixity, we suffer.

When teaching the three marks of existence, the Buddha assigned his students an observation exercise similar to Professor Roberts's. He sent his disciples to meditate not in an art gallery but in a charnel ground, instructing them to observe corpses in their various stages of decomposition—

... one, two, or three days dead, bloated, livid, and oozing matter... being devoured by crows, hawks, vultures, dogs, jackals, or various kind of worms... a skeleton with flesh and blood, held together with sinews... a fleshless skeleton smeared with blood, held together with sinews... a skeleton without flesh and blood, held together with sinews... disconnected bones scattered in all directions... bones bleached white, the color of shells... bones heaped up, more than a year old... bones rotten and crumbling to dust...*

You get the picture. Buddha's strategy was to force his students to confront what scared and disgusted them so that they could *see* reality at

---

* Mahasatipatthana Sutta, vi. Navasivathika Pabba [Section on Nine Stages of Corpses].

work and thereby understand the truth of the three marks of existence. This dose of reality, he hoped, would liberate them from the suffering caused by their delusory attachment to what was not fixed, permanent, or real.

My face is not a work of art, but neither is it ready for the charnel ground, yet. Meditating upon it for three hours, however painful, is not quite equivalent to what the Buddha suggests, but then again my goals are more modest. I'm not looking for liberation or enlightenment. I'm just trying to write this essay about my face, and making a time log seemed like a good place to start. And since it is a meditative exercise, I decided to conduct the experiment in front of the small Buddhist altar where I meditate every day. I sat down on my cushion and looked at the mirror where the statue of the Buddha should be, feeling stupid and vaguely transgressive. Buddhism is a nontheistic religion. There is nothing inherently holy about a statue of Buddha. Buddha is not a god. Buddhism teaches that we are *all* buddhas because we all have buddha nature. This being so, replacing the Buddha with a mirror and gazing into it should, theoretically, be fine. A bit literal, perhaps, but doctrinally not a problem. So why do I feel so uncomfortable, like I'm committing an act of Zen sacrilege?

TIME CODE 00:10:12

00:10:12   Staring at my face, I'm aware that I want to touch it. Touch the scar on my forehead, the pimple on my chin, rub my nose, my eyes, scratch my cheek. I'm aware that everything looks wrong, my face, my hair, my collar, and I want to fix things. I run my fingers through my hair, pulling it back from my face. It falls forward again like a curtain. It's trying to shield me from myself. Nice. I've spent much of my life hiding behind this curtain of hair.

00:13:02   When I look myself in the eye, it's hard to look away. Eyes define a face. If we were not such visual creatures, if we received our sensory input some other way, maybe we would not need faces. Trees do not need faces. Jellyfish do not need faces. Daisies do, and they don't have eyes, so perhaps I am wrong about this.

00:14:37 Still watching the eyes. Sad. Serious. Brown. Slanting downward. The angle of the slope seems more pronounced, more acute than I'd realized. Have my eyes changed? My eyelids are heavier. The folds of skin almost meet the lashes. The right eye and left eye are very different. The left eye looks slightly more Asiatic. The right epicanthic fold is more pronounced, making that eye look more Caucasian. I used to notice this when I put on eyeliner. But here's something I've never noticed before, or at least never admitted: I have a preference. It's subtle, but I've always preferred my right eye to my left. I've preferred my Caucasian eye to my Asian eye. Strange.

OPTICAL ORIENTATION

When I was growing up, we all knew that Orientals had slanty eyes. We knew that Chinese eyes slanted upwards and Japanese eyes slanted downwards. In school, we used to play a game about this. Putting our fingers in the outside corners of our eyes, we'd push them up and sing *Chinee!* Then we'd pull them down and sing *Japanee!* And then, pushing one corner up and pulling the other down, canting our eyes in different directions and making them wonky, we'd holler, *Half-n-half!* I hollered louder than anyone, because I was the punch line. Everyone knew it, and this made me feel special—a little uneasy and a little bit proud.

Nothing about the joke or the punch line was true, of course. Chinese eyes did not go up, Japanese eyes did not go down, my eyes did not go in opposite directions, and I wasn't half-Chinee. My father was Caucasian American, of Anglo-Saxon and northern European descent. My mother was ethnically Japanese and had been a Japanese citizen, although by the time I was born she'd become a naturalized American. On my birth certificate, my father's race is recorded as "white" and my mother's race as "yellow."

I grew up thinking of myself as half-Japanese, although the word "half" used to confuse me. Half of what? Which half was which, and how was I divided? Was Japanese the top half or the bottom? Or did the dividing line run diagonally? Once, when I was about ten or eleven, some boys accosted me in a park and asked me if I had a slanty Jap vagina. That confused me, too. I'd never heard the word vagina spoken out loud before.

Growing up in Connecticut, I never thought myself half-white or half-American. White American was the default, so that half never needed to be articulated. White American was not comical or joke-worthy, and there was no need to point fingers at it.

As kids, were we aware of the underlying racism of our games? I think not, or not entirely. We just thought it was funny to distort our faces into caricature, squashing our cheeks and crossing our eyes, making Asian buck teeth, Negro lips, and piggy noses. Our faces were young and pliable, and we stretched and twisted our features like Silly Putty, testing the grotesque plasticity of self. We laughed. We were hilarious. Nobody stopped us. Words like *Chinee* and *Japanee* were just part of the postwar lexicon, and somehow we knew they were meant to be comical, while other words, like *Chink*, *Jap*, *Nip*, or *nigger* were not.

But even though we may not have been fully conscious of the racism of our games, we did understand that racial stereotyping was titillating and a little bit taboo. And as a *half*, my understanding went deeper. In some preconscious and inchoate way, I felt the precarious instability that comes with the mixing of blood. I understood that identity is fluid, that it exists on a spectrum, and that to some extent, I had a choice about where I fell. So when the kids contorted their faces, although I felt uneasy at being identified with the wonky half-n-half face, I suspect I also felt relieved and even grateful that as a diluted yellow person, the peril I represented was only half what it might be. And so, in order to align myself further with the hegemony and keep the real bad words at bay, I raised my voice and joined the chorus, pulling my eyes out of shape and singing out *Chinee... Japanee...* The trick, I learned, was to appropriate the punch line.

Here was another game we played: When the first snow dusted the ground, my best friend Jane and I would get long sticks and go out into the street and use the sticks to draw faces. I would draw Japanese faces, and Jane would draw American faces. The game we were playing was World War II, and these faces were our troops. The person with the most troops would win the war. We'd draw our faces in the same way, with a big circle for the head, dots for the nose, and a line for the mouth. Only the eyes were different. Mine were just two slants, slashed quickly in the snow, but Jane had to draw whole little circles for eyes, which took her a lot longer, and since it was a race, she always lost. We'd play until dusk and the entire street was filled with faces and my Japan had won. It never occurred to us that we were rewriting history.

TIME CODE 00:17:28

00:17:28   I've always felt a bit funny wearing eyeliner, like it's cheating, a betrayal of who I am, to try and make my eyes look bigger. And mascara, too. I have skimpy Asian eyelashes, so what's the point?

00:19:02   I'm feeling pretty idiotic right now. This experiment is ridiculous. Narcissistic. Solipsistic. Banal. I don't want to do it anymore. Isn't it time for coffee?

00:20:46   Deep breath. Bring the mind back. Try again. Don't look away. What do I spy now?

Heavy bags under my eyes. Saggy, slightly puffy. Baggage from my dad. I first started noticing them in my late thirties and they horrified me. I didn't want to look like my dad. Didn't want to see his reproachful, drooping, disappointed gaze staring back at me every time I looked in the mirror. But there was nothing I could do about it. The bags were there. They were the most conspicuous part of my face. It's possible no one else noticed them, but I could not look at my face and not see them. I think I started wearing thick-framed glasses around then.

00:24:32   Strange. Just realized that I haven't paid much attention to the bags for several years now. I mean, I see them when I look, but I don't obsess about them anymore. What's changed? Certainly not the bags themselves. If anything, they've only gotten worse. Have I just gotten used to them? Or is it that my feelings about my dad have changed? He's been dead for more than fifteen years now. The grief and anguish I felt at his death have softened, and when I see his eyes in mine, I don't see reproach or disappointment anymore. Instead of judgment, I see concern, watchfulness, maybe even a kind of compassionate discernment. So this is better, an improvement! I don't mind meeting him here in the mirror. It's kind of nice. Hey, Dad. How are you doing?

ORIGINAL FACE

What did your face look like before your parents were born?

Zen koans are little allegorical nuggets designed to break your head on. They are ancient *Gedankenexperiments*, the dogged contemplation of which promises to lead to enlightenment, only unlike Western philosophical thought experiments, koans don't operate rationally. They are more like no-thought experiments, whose potency lies in their ability to break through rigid, dualistic mental habits and go beyond the limitations of the rational, interpretive mind. Still, the habit of interpretation dies hard, and over the centuries, Zen teachers have written extensive commentaries on the koan literature.

So what does this koan mean? According to the thirteenth-century Zen master, Eihei Dōgen,* "your face before your parents were born" is your true face, your originally enlightened buddha nature. A second version of this koan asks, *Without thinking good or evil, what is your original face?* In essence, the two koans ask the same question: What are you? What is your true self, your undivided nature? What is your identity before and beyond these kinds of dualistic distinctions, like father-mother and good-evil, that define us?

*

* Dōgen Zenji (道元禅師; also Dōgen Kigen 道元希玄, or Eihei Dōgen 永平道元) (1200–1253), founder of the Sōtō school of Zen Buddhism.

I was born in 1956, eleven years after the end of World War II, when Americans were still good, the Japanese were still evil, and a nondualistic understanding was not yet possible. Eleven years prior to my birth, my two halves had been mortal enemies. My mother's people were killing my father's people, and vice versa, and at a very young age, I was aware of this enmity and aware, too, that I embodied it. And yet my face evinced its opposite: the force of the attraction—true love, sex, miscegenation, call it what you will—that brought me into being. With all these primal and contrary passions eddying below the surface of my skin, it's no wonder people found my face disturbing.

In a racially and ethnically segregated society like America in the 1950s and '60s, there is no way to look at the face of a mixed-race person and not be immediately reminded of sex and difference. The association might be subliminal, but our brains are hardwired for pattern recognition, and when we spot a deviation from the pattern, our instinct is to parse the hows and whys. But thoughts of sex and difference often feel transgressive, especially when occasioned by the face of a child. Mixed-race children make adults uneasy. We make people behave in odd ways.

When I was little, complete strangers used to come up to me on the street and peer into my face and ask, *What* are *you?* Curious, aggressive, prurient, or naive, they couldn't help themselves. They were responding to something in my features that was so existentially unsettling it excused even rudeness, but even so, it was my face that was at fault. In its refusal to resolve into one thing or another, my face was the occasion for their discomfort.

She is nother fyshe nor fleshe, nor good red hearyng.

Half, hybrid, mulatto, chimera... in the uncanny valley, ordinary manners do not apply.

Demographics have changed, and now there are many more mixed-race people in the world, but in the 1950s and '60s, we were more of an anomaly. And identity politics were still emerging, so the language we used was not as skillful, sensitive, or precise. Now people think twice before asking *What* are *you?* They find some other way to ask. But back then we had less awareness of the racism inherent in the question, and perhaps a greater tolerance for its clumsiness, too.

My parents never seemed to mind or take offense. They were both linguists, and they understood the human love of taxonomies and our need to identify, classify, and pin down meaning with words.

My dad taught in the Department of Anthropology at Yale, and back then his colleagues were all white men.* New Haven didn't have a large Asian community at the time, and the only Asians I knew were like my mom, the wives of the white, male anthropologists. In fact, it became kind of a joke that in order to get tenure in the Yale Department of Anthropology you had to have an Oriental wife. "Oriental" was what we used to call Asian people back then, and it was mostly the Oriental wives themselves who thought this joke was funny. They formed kind of a strange demographic subset, these exotic Oriental wives of anthropologists, as did we, their half-Oriental, half-anthropological children.

Growing up then, I was both the observer and the observed, both self and other. Half-Asian and

---

* The first female full professor was hired at Yale in 1970.

half-anthropologist, is it surprising that I should now find myself sitting in front of a mirror, studying my face? The predilection for voyeurism, for this kind of ethnographic introspection, is in my genes.

TIME CODE 00:34:12

00:34:12   Okay, let's move on to my forehead, which is HUGE. I have an exceedingly broad and spacious forehead, which again I got from my dad, who truly needed a lot of office space to house his big brain. On me, it's overkill. The skin's become a bit papery, and there are some fine horizontal lines, but overall it's still pretty smooth.

00:39:49   I have two scars on my forehead. The little one, which is hidden under my hairline, I got when my friend and I were fencing, and he hit me with a broom pole. The big scar, which runs vertically down the right side of my forehead, I got in a sledding accident behind the Yale Divinity School when I was in the third grade.

I'd never been sledding at the Divinity School before, but I was playing with some of the other faculty kids from the Department of Anthropology, and they told me it was okay. The hill was crazy steep, and I remember looking down and feeling scared, but instead of backing away, I lay on my sled, belly down, and a moment later I was careening headfirst, straight toward the wrought-iron fence at the bottom. I remember the slick ice under the runners, and the jaw-breaking bumps, and the terror of knowing I was not in control, but it was all happening so fast and there was nothing I could do, and then the fence was there, and I crashed into it.

I remember the taste of the iron. I remember red blood on white snow. So much blood. Two Divinity School graduate students ran down the hill to rescue me. They carried me back up to their apartment and then drove me to the emergency room, where my mother met us. The doctor put twenty-four stitches in my forehead and sewed my upper lip back together. You can barely see either scar now. My mother thanked the Divinity School students and told everyone how lucky it was that they were there to save me. Is that when my interest in religions started? Later that week, I was supposed to be in the school play. We were doing *The Mikado*, and because I was half-Japanese, I'd been cast as Yum-Yum, the leading female role, which was a very big deal because I was only eight. I didn't care about the sledding accident or my split lip or the stitches to my head. All I cared about was whether I would still be able to play Yum-Yum.

Could this be true? Is it possible that in 1964, my elementary school would put on a production of *The Mikado*? With all of its anachronistic Orientalisms and racial stereotypes, it seems like an unlikely opera to do with children, but why else would I know these songs that Yum-Yum sings with Pitti-Sing and Peep-Bo?

> *Three little maids from school are we,*
> *Pert as a school-girl well can be,*
> *Filled to the brim with girlish glee,*
> *Three little maids from school!*

> *Everything is a source of fun.*
> *Nobody's safe, for we care for none!*
> *Life is a joke that's just begun!*
> *Three little maids from school!*

And I do recall prancing around a stage in a kimono, twirling a parasol, so I must have recovered enough from the accident to do the play.

After that I grew bangs to hide my big, scarred forehead, and I kept the bangs for most of my life, long after the scar faded. But even before the accident, I didn't like my forehead. It was too big, too broad, and too masculine—a fine forehead for my father, but not for me.

JUMPERS

My father's paternal ancestors came to America from Yorkshire, England, and his maternal ancestors came from Denmark. The Yorkshire branch of the family were early settlers and fought on both sides of the American Revolutionary War; after the British lost, the Tory side moved to Canada. My father's parents were dairy farmers in Wisconsin, but they went bankrupt during the Great Depression and were forced to sell the farm to a large agribusiness conglomerate. The loss of the farm just about broke their hearts, and they turned to religion for comfort and became evangelical Christians. Most people have heard of the

Shakers and the Quakers and the Holy Rollers, who shake and quake and roll. My father's family were Jumpers.

It sounds like fun, but it wasn't. The Jumpers were a very strict, conservative, fundamentalist Christian sect who considered everything fun a sin. In old family portraits, my paternal ancestors stare dourly down at me from their carved oval frames. They have great wide foreheads and small blue eyes, thin lips and narrow jaws. *What are you?* their eyes seem to ask. I never know what to answer.

And yet, when my parents married five years after the end of the war, my father's parents welcomed their new Japanese daughter-in-law unreservedly. My Japanese grandparents, on the other hand, were not so accepting. They'd hoped my mother would marry a nice Japanese boy, so it took some convincing, but eventually my father won them over, and until the day she died, my Japanese grandmother talked about what a good, kind man my father was.

TIME CODE 00:49:02

00:49:02   Not to obsess about the bags under my eyes, but they just reminded me of a funny story. On my first book tour, I think it was in Denver, I had a literary escort whose husband was a pilot, and she told me that the pilots and flight attendants put hemorrhoid cream on the bags under their eyes. Preparation H, I think it was. It has some active ingredient that supposedly shrinks swelling, but I never tried it, so I don't know if it works. The escort said that by the time her authors got to Denver, they were exhausted and worn out by touring and looked like shit, but when they left Denver, they looked ten years younger.

I love the idea of all these exhausted authors applying Preparation H to their faces. I think it's funny, but why? I mean, rationally, I understand there's nothing inherently unclean or unsanitary about hemorrhoid cream, so why not put it on your face? What makes a face so special? It's just an organizational device. A planar surface housing a cluster of holes, a convenient gathering place for the sense organs. Makes a lot of sense from a design perspective to put the sense organs up high, where the vista is greater, and all on one side, preferably the side oriented in the direction you're likely to be traveling so you can see what's coming, sniff out food, listen for danger. Good to locate them near the cerebellum so the neural signals don't have to travel so far. Good to put the mouth near the eyes and nose, and the nose away from the asshole.

00:53:47 Hmph. Dad is looking out at me reproachfully again. He doesn't like the turn things have taken. Doesn't like me talking about assholes. He thinks it's rude, not in good taste.

00:54:12 More projection. It's taken me a long time to get over my fear of disappointing him—and apparently I still haven't. If I still see his disappointment in my eyes, I must still be carrying some of that fear. Maybe I always will. And maybe it's not such a bad thing, either. His gaze still has the power to make me feel uncomfortable, but maybe it makes me careful, too.

SILENCE

It was so hard to put my first film out into the world, to publish my first novel, to break my family's silence. I suspect all families have this, some code of silence that is absolute and inviolable and yet so omnipresent as to be almost invisible, too. Like God. Or air.

My father, shy and shamed by his fundamentalist Christian upbringing, was the obvious source of our silence, but my mother was complicit, forfeiting her own words to protect his sensibilities, lapsing into stoic silence, too. Saving face. As a Japanese woman, saving face came naturally to her.

She used to like to write letters to the editors of the various newspapers and magazines she read, and since she was a good writer, her letters were sometimes published, which made her proud, but then for some reason she stopped. Much later, after my father's death, she explained why. It seems he told her that seeing her letters in print, with his name (her married name) attached, embarrassed him. He asked her not to write them anymore.

I was surprised and shocked to hear this. Somewhat ruefully, she defended him. He was a very private man and had his reputation to think about, she said, as if that explained anything. I still didn't get it. He was a distinguished international scholar, renowned in his field. How could my mother's paragraph-long letter to the editor at *Time* magazine, praising their choice for Man of the Year, damage my father's reputation? Was it her opinion he objected to, or the fact that she had one? Was it her choice of venue? Was *Time* magazine too lowbrow? My dad wasn't a snob. He was a good, kind man, generous, gentle, and fair-minded, and everyone said so. The only explanation I can imagine is that the range of self-expression he could tolerate was so narrow that it choked off the possibility for those closest to him, his wife and daughter, to have a voice in the world.

When I was growing up, I wanted to be good, and I knew being good meant being reserved and private. This expectation was always implicit, but after I made my first film, my dad made it explicit. *Halving the Bones* was an autobiographical film about my Japanese grandparents, and before I released it, I showed it to my mom and dad. There were places in the film when I used fake footage and took liberties with documentary evidence in order to question the reliability of memory and "truth." I wanted to make sure my mom was okay with this, and also with the way I'd portrayed her and her parents. I wanted to get her blessing to take the film out into the world.

The three of us watched it together on our old television in my mom's study. I could tell that parts of it made her uncomfortable, and at times she didn't understand what I was trying to achieve, but in the end she said that she liked it and that it was fine for me to screen it publicly. My dad said he liked it, too, but later he pulled me aside. He said he didn't mind that I'd made a film about my mother's side of the family, but would I please not make films about him and his family? It was a formal request, and I could tell he was uncomfortable making it. He was embarrassed, and he didn't want to hurt my feelings. It pained him to have to make this request so explicit. Why couldn't I just know better?

Writing this, I'm aware that a reader might think we had some terrible family secret shrouded in the silence, but as far as I know, we didn't. Or, if such a secret source of shame existed, some original sin, it was inaccessible to me, hidden so far back in time that I could only feel its ripples.

I gave my dad my word. Of course I'm not making films anymore, and most of what I write is fiction, so this hasn't been a problem, but still I do try to be mindful of his feelings. When I write about him in an autobiographical context like this one, I try to be fair, to tell the truth as best I can, and to avoid cheap shots and rhetorical hyperbole. Increasingly, this applies to everything I write. As the years go by, his gaze in mine, which used to distress me, has become a source of stability and strength. Our tastes are different, but overall, I think he's helped me become a better writer. Good, kind, generous, and fair-minded, he's exactly the kind of person you'd want to read your work with a critical eye.

He never did read my first novel, *My Year of Meats*, though, and I never asked him to. He was sick by then and close to death, and there were things in the book—sex, violence, some bad language—that we both knew would cause him embarrassment and discomfort. But I described the book to him, and he liked the premise and what I was trying to do. He was proud of me, proud that I'd written a novel, proud that I was going to be a published author. He told me this. He told everyone. I asked him if publishing the book under his family name (my surname) would embarrass him, and he started to cry. He explained to me then that he was worried about his sister. She was old and still a devout fundamentalist Christian, and he didn't want to hurt or offend her. It sounds like an excuse, but I don't think it was. I believe he was telling the truth, as he saw it, although I also think that his sister, my aunt, was much tougher and more tolerant than he gave her credit for. I believe my dad would have been willing to suffer his own discomfort and embarrassment for my sake, but in the end I decided to spare us all by offering to use a pen name instead. "Ozeki" took care of the problem, and although forfeiting my name angered and saddened me, it was worth it. I could tell my dad was relieved. He died exactly one week before the book was published.

In the beginning of *My Year of Meats*, the parents of the protagonist, Jane Takagi-Little, argue about hyphenating her surname. Jane's father says, "It doesn't *mean* anything. It's just a *name*!" to which her Japanese mother replies, "How can you say '*justa name*'? Name is very *first* thing. Name is face to all the world."

Ozeki is not my father's face nor my mother's face, either. Ozeki is my face, the face I chose, a nominal face that keeps them safe from me, and me safe from them.

TIME CODE 00:55:43

00:55:43 I like my cheekbones. They are my mother's cheekbones, and her father's cheekbones. My maternal grandfather was very intense. He was a poet and a photographer and an artist, and he had all sorts of esoteric physical and mental regimens that he practiced, like standing barefoot on the blades of upturned swords and sticking metal skewers through his arms, in order to train his body and mind. He had awesome cheekbones, a square, strong, prominent jawline, and an aquiline nose. Piercing eyes. As I get older, sometimes I can see small glimpses of his face and my mother's in mine, and I like that.

ZEN

My maternal ancestors came from Japan and were Zen Buddhists. Zen Buddhists and Jumpers are very different in many ways, but the most obvious is this: Jumpers jump. Zen Buddhists sit. My very first memory is of my Japanese grandparents sitting zazen. I was three years old, and we lived in New Haven, Connecticut, and my grandparents were visiting us from Hawaii. My maternal grandfather was born in Hiroshima in 1880 and immigrated to Hawaii as an indentured laborer when he was sixteen years old. He worked on the sugarcane plantations, and when his contract was finished, he bought a camera and became the first official photographer for Hawai'i Volcanoes National Park. He must have done quite well for himself, because he was able to marry my grandmother, who was the daughter of an old samurai family, living in Tokyo. The marriage was arranged through an exchange of photographs, and looking at these portraits, it's easy to see why. My grandmother was beautiful, and my grandfather was strikingly handsome. He was a sumi-e painter, a haiku poet, and a photographer, living in an exotic island paradise. Looking at his chiseled face and piercing eyes, my grandmother must have thought he was very romantic. I certainly did.

I only met him that one time when I was three, but he made an impression. We lived in a tiny house with no guest room, so my grandparents slept in my parents' bedroom. They arrived at night, after I was asleep, and the next morning my mother sent me to call them for breakfast. I remember standing at the closed bedroom door. Maybe I knocked, or maybe I didn't. I remember feeling a sense of gravity mixed with confusion. I had been charged with a mission. What to do? I turned the knob and opened the door.

Nothing in my entire three years of life prepared me for what I saw. My grandmother and grandfather were sitting cross-legged on the floor, rocking gently back and forth. This was back in 1959, in Connecticut, at a time when adults did not sit cross-legged on the floor, so I remember this because it's unusual when you're three to see an adult who is your height, but there they were, at my eye level exactly, only their eyes were cast downward, and mine were wide open. But just then my grandfather looked up, and his eyes met mine, and in that moment of meeting, face-to-face, something passed between us. If

I were to depict it as a manga, I would draw a sparking blue arc of electricity, like a lightning bolt, traveling from his old eyes to mine.

I must have stood there for a while, transfixed, before backing out of the room and running into the kitchen to tell my mother what I'd seen. I imagine she tried to explain it to me, telling that they were sitting zazen, which meant nothing to a three-year-old, so she went and got my Daruma doll to demonstrate. "Daruma" is the Japanese name for Bodhidharma, the monk who brought the Zen lineage from India to China, and who is famous for sitting in silent meditation, gazing at a wall, for nine years. Japanese Daruma dolls are round and red and shaped like a rice ball, with no legs or arms and big, blank, white circles where their eyes should be. They often have a curved bottom so they rock, and the idea is that even if you push them over they'll always regain their balance.

So, my mom set my Daruma rocking back and forth, and she explained that this was zazen meditation, the same thing my grandma and grandpa were doing. She explained that Daruma had been a really good meditator, and in fact, he'd been such a good meditator and had meditated for so long that his arms and legs fell off. And the reason he had no eyes was that he had gotten sleepy while he was meditating and so he pulled off his eyelids and threw them on the ground, where they turned into a tea plant.

This was my introduction to my grandparents and to Zen. It's a wonder I didn't choose to jump instead.

TIME CODE 00:57:26

00:57:26 I am exercising my eyebrows, raising them skeptically, furrowing them into a frown. Never realized this before, but I like my left eyebrow more than my right. It's quizzical. It has an ironic arch, but oddly, I can't control it as well as the right one. The muscles on that side seem a little lazy, like I'm an asymmetrical marionette with a broken eyebrow string. My eyebrows are thinning. I used to pluck them to give them a nice shape, but I don't anymore. What if they disappear altogether? I don't want to be an old lady who has to draw in her eyebrows with a pencil... but then again, screw it, why the hell not?

OBSESSIONS

It's surprising I have any eyebrows left at all. When I was a child, I suffered from trichotillomania, or hair-pulling disorder. I used to pull out my eyebrows and eyelashes and split the ends of my hair, making collections of the small, curled leavings on a white page or on the ivory keys of the piano when I was supposed to be doing homework or practicing. Trichotillomania seems to lie somewhere on the spectrum of obsessive-compulsive disorders, and the peak age of onset is between nine and thirteen, which was exactly when my own compulsions started. The behavior is often triggered by depression or stress, which the ritual of hair-pulling relieves.

I grew out of the habit of eyebrow and eyelash pulling, but split ends continued to be my dark obsession. Frozen and silent, I deconstructed them for hours, developing an elaborate taxonomy of the types and ways that hairs could split. Some were simply bifurcated in the shape of a Y, while others were more like feathers, multiple and finely branched, and these were the prize because they presented the greatest challenge. The trick was to grasp each individual barb and pull it for as long as possible up the shaft until it came loose. I can remember even now the trance-like state, the tension in my body as I performed these minute operations, and the shame I felt, sensing this behavior was wrong and sick, but unable to stop myself. I was an emotional and secretive child.

It wasn't that hair-splitting relieved my anxiety, exactly. It was more that by engaging in this ritual, I was able to control the tension and hold it locked in my body so I wouldn't explode. Eventually, in my teens, I cured myself of trichotillomania by cutting off my hair and learning how to smoke and drink—self-medicating rituals which I performed just as compulsively for decades.

These kinds of obsessive compulsions are not uncommon. High schools are filled with hunched, cross-eyed girls, enthralled with splitting the ends of their hair. In Japan, I used to see them on the subway all the time. Some of the girls clipped off the split ends with tiny nail scissors, which they carried in their handbags solely for that purpose. Nowadays, you don't see this kind of thing as much. Now they're all compulsively texting or playing games on their smartphones instead.

TIME CODE 01:00:19

01:00:19 Finally! An hour has passed. Lick your lips. Blow yourself a kiss and get on with it.

01:01:14 Do I really have to sit here for another two hours? What an insane idea this was…

01:02:38 Ooh, nice frown! Scary. As I get older, my expressions seem to have gotten more exaggerated and severe. Obviously, I'm not always aware of what my face is doing, but I suspect its habitual expression these days is a frown or a scowl. When I'm on book tours, I get photographed a lot, and while I do my best not to look at pictures and videos afterward, I can't help noticing that I'm often caught with really frightening expressions on my face—expressions that look like disdain, or disapproval, or contempt, when I'm probably just thinking about what I want to eat for dinner. Old people look scary. I don't want to look scary. I don't want others to feel despised or scorned. Maybe I should try to cultivate a milder countenance. Practice mindfulness of the face. Be inscrutable. Mask-like and Oriental. Cultivate an enigmatic smile. I can see why people get Botox.

MASKS

When I was young, my half-Japanese face signified a self that was at odds with who I felt myself to be. My face was a surface onto which people, especially men, projected their ideas of race and sexuality, Asian-ness and femininity, ideas that had little or nothing to do with me. I grew up wearing a mask on my face that I didn't know was there, but over the years, of course, the mask shaped me.

I turned fourteen in 1970. The image of Asian girls as exotic, ageless, child sex objects was still very much a part of the post-World War II, post-Korean War, post-Vietnam War culture in America. These Asian wars had created a persistent sexual stereotype. Asian girls were Other, and men who might have refrained from having sex with a fourteen-year-old white girl who looked like their sister or daughter felt less inhibition with me. During my teenage years, I had several relationships with these older men, who often held positions of power and authority and were supposed to be responsible for my well-being. These relationships never felt real, because the "I" who was having them never felt real. That "I" desperately wanted to be different from me. That "I" allowed things to happen because that's what was expected of her. That "I" was the mask, and she was having the relationships.

The iconic Japanese Noh mask, called the *ko-omote*, depicts a young girl of about fourteen or fifteen. She has a round white face, full cheeks, and lustrous white skin that is almost pearlescent. Her hair is parted demurely in the center, and the lines of her eyes are graceful and long, slanting up just slightly at the outer corners. Her mouth is small, and her plump bow-shaped lips are parted in an enigmatic smile so that her blackened teeth peek out seductively. In Japan, for centuries it was customary for women to blacken their teeth and to pluck out their eyebrows and paint them on again about an inch or so above the natural brow line. The ko-omote's wide eyebrows look like a pair of inky thumbprints, set high on her forehead, just below her hairline. They slope slightly down at the edges, which give her a look that is bemused, quizzical, and gently expectant, like she's waiting for you to do something delightful, but would be equally happy if you did something foolish.

We think of masks as being expressionless, but what's marvelous about the ko-omote is the subtle range of emotion she can convey. Her face, which is slightly asymmetrical, exhibits an ideal called *chūkan hyōjō*, which means an ambiguous expression, neutral beauty, or versatile vagueness. By slightly raising or dipping his chin, tilting his head, or favoring one side, a skilled actor—and, by tradition, professional Noh actors are male*—can express feelings of joy or grief or anger or uncertainty. In the absence of the actor's face, the mask becomes the medium for emotion.

After I graduated from college, I went to Japan to do graduate work in classical Japanese

---

* This is changing. According to the article "Women in Noh" by Eric Prideaux from the April 11th, 2004 issue of the *Japan Times*, there are about 250 female Noh professionals in Japan, comprising a sixth of the total of 1,540 professional performers.

literature at Nara Women's University. I had studied Shakespeare as an undergraduate, and my idea was now to read Zeami, the fourteenth-century Japanese playwright of the Noh theater. Since the performance of Noh was so foreign to me, I decided to take lessons in Noh chanting and dance in Kyoto with Udaka Michishige.* Noh is one of Japan's National Intangible Cultural Properties, and as a government-designated representative, Udaka is now considered to be a living national treasure. He was one of the first actors to welcome foreigners to study along with his Japanese students, and the only Noh actor who is also a master carver of masks.

These lessons were my first encounter with the Zen arts, and even though Udaka-sensei didn't speak explicitly about Zen, its spirit infused the

* Udaka Michishige's biography is available at internationalnohinstitute.wordpress.com.

dojo and our practice. Noh is a meditation of sound and movement. The ritualistic elements of performance—the slow sonorous chanting, hypnotic dance, music, and drums—work to animate the mask, which comes to life in a moment of sublime beauty called *yūgen*. In his book, *The Secrets of Noh Masks*, Udaka writes about yūgen:

> It refers, I suppose, to a sort of mysterious, unfathomable aesthetic quality, but even that is uncertain... No matter how much you rehearse, it remains elusive, slipping constantly from your grasp. It's a complex sensation, impossible to describe exactly... Complex, but, oh, with such lingering sweetness!*

---

* Michishige Udaka, *The Secrets of Noh Masks* (Tokyo: Kodansha International, 2010), 7.

Ineffable and elusive, evanescent and eternal, yūgen is the most profound expression of the Japanese aesthetic experience. Udaka writes, "In the subtle interplay of light and shadow in Noh masks lives the yūgen of Noh: the legacy of Zeami."[*]

I'd always been fascinated with masks, and so I joined Udaka-sensei's mask carving class. The first mask I made was a ko-omote, a challenging mask because of the enigmatic complexities of her expression, which must convey both her naïve innocence as well as a hint of the unforgiving sharpness of her youthful character. Udaka writes, "The section from the eyelids to the bridge of the nose must be especially plain and devoid of affectation, requiring the maskmaker to rid his mind of worldly thoughts."[†] No easy task.

---

[*] Udaka, *The Secrets of Noh Masks*, 9.

[†] Udaka, *The Secrets of Noh Masks*, 12.

Noh masks are carved from a type of Japanese cypress called hinoki. The best wood comes from trees that are over 250 years old, and which, after felling, are cured for another forty or fifty years, resulting in a block of wood that will not bend or crack. The mask is buried in the block of wood, and it's the carver's job to release it. First the shape of the face is roughed out with a mallet and chisel, and then, with the aid of a series of cardboard templates, the carver slowly refines the features using a variety of smaller chisels, knives, and sandpaper. The inside of the mask is as important as the outside, since the shape of the interior affects the resonance and projection of the actor's voice. The mask thus functions like a musical instrument, merging with and enhancing the actor's chanting.

Once the face is done, the carver painstakingly finishes the mask with layer upon layer of fine paint made from powdered mother-of-pearl shell mixed with an animal-derived glue, which gives the mask its pearlescent and lustrous white complexion. Each thin coat of paint must be applied, dried, and sanded before the next goes on, and dozens of coats are required. After the base is laid, color is applied using mineral pigments, red to the lips, black to the teeth and the hair and the eyes, and a subtle range of ochers to the dips and contours of the face, bringing out its highlights and shadows. Painting the hair is particularly exacting. It demands a steady hand and intense focus and concentration, since the placement of each strand can change the character of the mask.

The process of carving and painting and polishing a mask can take up to a year. The final step is the aging of the mask. This is not an attempt to falsify or make a fake antique. Rather, it's a way of paying homage to the passage of time by evoking the qualities of *wabi-sabi*, another key element in Japanese aesthetics, which describes the beauty of things that are imperfect, impermanent, and incomplete.* The word *wabi*, meaning "proud" or "lonely," refers to qualities of subdued grace and austere simplicity, of dignity in the midst of privation. *Sabi* comes from *sabireru*, meaning "to become desolate," and is also a homonym for the word meaning "rust." Sabi describes the beauty and pathos of impermanence—the transient nature of all things—as well as the beautiful patina that objects acquire as they age. Together, wabi and sabi evoke the aching appreciation of the beauty of the moment, which arises from our human awareness that everything in life is transient. Wabi-sabi is the aesthetic expression

---

* Leonard Koren, *Wabi-Sabi for Artists, Designers, Poets and Philosophers*, (Berkeley, CA: Stone Bridge Press, 1994), 7.

of the Zen teaching of the three marks of existence: suffering, impermanence, and no-self. This deeply philosophical aesthetic awareness is part of the beauty of Noh masks, even the young ko-omote.

Udaka-sensei taught us various techniques to age and distress the faces of the masks. Using a very small brush, with a tip no larger than a single hair, he would painstakingly outline the lips and stain the creases around the nose with faint fine lines of sepia, creating shadows of discoloration. The masks are attached to the actor's face using silk cords threaded through holes on the sides of the masks where the ears would be. Over time, the cords of a venerable and well-used mask will rub against the paint and wear it down, so Udaka-sensei used a fine sandpaper to create this abrasion. Another technique he called *mushi-kui*, or "bug-eating." The animal-based gelatin glue used to bind the powdered mother-of-pearl is delicious to certain insects, which burrow into the ancient masks, leaving behind wormlike trails around the outer edges and hairline. Sensei taught us how to replicate these insect trails, digging into the paint with a small sharp knife, and, at the risk of sounding like I'm bragging, mushi-kui was my forte.

Aging a mask's face is a daunting task. You've been working on it for up to a year, and finally, just as it's nearing perfection, you have to make it imperfect again, but perfectly so. Perfectly imperfect. Often students would balk at doing mushi-kui, and then Udaka-sensei would send them to me. *Ask Ruth*, he'd say. *Mushi-kui ga umai.** Every person has her own small talent, and I was proud of mine. To achieve an authentic-seeming

---

* "Her bug-eating is excellent."

bug trail requires utter concentration, exacting precision, as well as a sharp eye, steady hand, and an intuitive understanding of distress and decay. These were skills I had honed since my childhood, through the painstaking splitting of hairs.

TIME CODE 01:05:24

01:05:24 Look at something long enough and it becomes strange. Repeat a word over and over and it becomes nonsense. Is this what's happening to my face? I can't see the whole anymore, only the smallest details. Defamiliarization... decomposition... disintegration... dissociation. Is this a path to madness?

01:07:52 Making familiar things strange is the job of the artist.

01:08:13 Focus on the details, then. I have a tiny scar on my right cheek. I don't know where it comes from. Chicken pox?

01:09:07   I have a tiny mole below my lip, on the left side of my mouth. Mom called it a beauty mark. She said actresses had them. Even Marilyn Monroe had one, so it was okay, but I never believed her. I didn't look like any actress I'd ever seen.

When I was twelve, Zeffirelli's *Romeo and Juliet* came out, and I fell madly in love with the sixteen-year-old actress who played Juliet.* My friend Jane said I looked like her. I desperately wanted this to be true, and there was enough of a resemblance to give me hope. The actress was half, too, although half-what I don't remember. She had long, wild, dark hair like mine. I saw the movie several times and learned her scenes by heart. That's how I fell in love with Shakespeare.

---

*   The half-British, half-Argentine actress, Olivia Hussey.

PRINCESS UPSIDE-DOWN HAIR

I still have the two masks I carved in Japan, a ko-omote, the young girl, and a *semimaru*, a mask that takes its name from one of the most tragic plays in the Noh repertoire. Semimaru depicts a blind young aristocrat, with a pale visage and eyes that are just the merest slits, downcast and unseeing. Oddly, though, Semimaru is not the lead role in the play that takes his name. That part is played by his sister, Princess Sakagami, or Princess Unruly Hair, which is more literally translated as Princess Upside-down Hair. Their story is simple. Blind from birth, Semimaru is a prince, who for some unknown reason has been banished by his father, the Emperor Daigo, to a distant mountain pass. He is accompanied there by a loyal attendant, who shaves his master's head in priestly tonsure, and then, after much lamenting, abandons the young prince in a grass hut, where he will live alone, with only his lute for company.

Banishment from the capital is a tragic cliché in Japanese narrative, but in this story, Semimaru is a far less tragic figure than the mad Princess Upside-down Hair. She enters the stage wearing not the ko-omote of a young girl in the blush of youth, but the mask of *zō-onna*, a slightly older woman, whose face has lost its plumpness and whose gaze has turned inward and melancholy. Refined, solemn, and otherworldly, the mask is often used to portray a celestial being or goddess who keeps a certain distance from the human realm. She is my favorite mask, and one that, according to Udaka, "demands a certain nobility of character in the maker."

Sakagami sings,

> *Though born a princess, some deed of evil*
> *From my unknown past in former lives*
> *Causes my mind at times to act deranged.*
> *And in my madness I wander distant ways.*
> *My blue-black hair grows skywards;*
> *Though I stroke it, it will not lie flat.**

Village children laugh at her upside-down hair, and she berates them, fending them off and then lapsing into a wonderful philosophical monologue about the inverted and non-dualistic nature of reality, a riff that is pure Zen.

---

* Zeami Motokiyo, *Semimaru*, trans. by Susan Matisoff, in *Twenty Plays of the Nō Theater*, edited by Donald Keene and Royall Tyler, (New York: Columbia University Press, 1970).

How extraordinary it is that
so much before our eyes is upside down.
Flower seeds buried in the ground rise up
to grace the branches of a thousand trees.
The moon hangs high in the heavens,
but its light sinks to the bottom of countless waters.

My hair, rising upward from my body,
Turns white with the touch of stars and frost:
The natural order or upside down?
How amazing that both should be within me!

[She enters the stage.]

The wind combs even the willows' hair
But neither can the wind untangle,
Nor my hand separate this hair.

[She takes hold of her hair and looks at it.]

Shall I rip it from my head? Throw it away?
I lift my sleeved hands—what is this?
The hair-tearing dance? How demeaning!

Mad and deranged, she begins to dance the hair-tearing dance as the chorus chants, telling of her many travails and hardships and ending with a description of her arrival at the same mountain pass where her brother has been left. Sakagami hears the sound of a lute coming from a grass hovel, and she recognizes her brother's elegant style of playing, so out of place in these rude surroundings. She approaches and recognizes Semimaru, and he recognizes her. Joyously they speak each other's names, profess their love for one another, and weep at the cruel turn of fate that has brought them to this pass. They share memories of the fine life they used to live at court, and then for no apparent reason, Sakagami announces she must go. Their leave-taking is drawn-out and tragic. She turns, hesitates, walks, pauses, calls back to him, then turns again to go. Her voice grows distant. He entreats her to visit him again, taking a few steps forward and turning his blind eyes in her direction. The chorus sings,

> *She turns a final time to look at him.*
> *Weeping, weeping they have parted,*
> *Weeping, weeping they have parted.*

There's no talk of Sakagami moving in with her blind brother, or of Semimaru caring for his mad sister or even helping her fix her hair. Their parting is a narrative requirement of the genre, and they simply accept it as necessary and inevitable, giving them the occasion to lament their loneliness, the pain of separation, and the tragic impermanence of the human condition.

The part of the play I find the most moving comes just after Sakagami's mad hair-tearing dance, before she hears her brother's lute. She arrives at the mountain pass and pauses by a stream.

In the running stream I see my reflection.
Though my own face, it horrifies me:
Hair like tangled briers crowns my head
Eyebrows blackly twist—yes, that is really
Sakagami's reflection in the water.
Water, they say, is a mirror,
But twilight ripples distort my face.

TIME CODE 01:13:57

01:13:57   Okay, now I really need a coffee break. Now.

01:24:21   Back again, with a cup of coffee. Made it with the new Hario, a really great Japanese coffee dripper for pour-over coffee that Oliver bought in a shop in Venice Beach. The ceramic dripper has special Japanese troughs, designed in a spiral to ensure an even and maximum extraction. Why am I writing this? Because I'm seriously bored with my face.

01:26:34 When I drink, my eyes squint and my eyebrows contract, creating two deep frown lines. The skin on my cheeks pulls upward, forming an array of crow's feet. Where did that phrase come from? Wrinkles do look like the feet or perhaps the toes of a crow. But why not a wren's foot? Or a bluebird's? Crow sounds like crone, that must be why. I have too many wrinkles for a single foot. I need many feet, many toes. I need a flock of crows. A murder of crows. A murder of crones.

01:29:06 Now I am making stupid faces at myself in the mirror. Sad faces, happy faces. Grimaces and grins. Drawing down the corners of my lips, sticking out my jaw, crossing my eyes. Sucking in my cheeks and making a kissy goldfish mouth. Grinning like a death's head. I have big white teeth. Can I check my email now?

01:31:12 I used to practice faces in the mirror. My friend Molly says she has a "mirror face," and I do, too. Funny. Like we're trying to fool ourselves into thinking we look better than we do. Who are we pretending to? These days we all have selfie faces. So funny to watch people taking selfies.

01:33:27 Age spots along my jawline, but I don't notice them very often, since they're on the side of my face. They don't really bother me, but the ruddiness of my skin does. I wear a light foundation when I have to be photographed. I don't like it. I don't really know how to put on makeup. I learned once but never practiced. When I was getting ready for my first book tour, I went to a high-end cosmetic store and asked them to teach me how to put on makeup. It was Shu Uemura, on West Broadway. I went away with a couple hundred dollars worth of product, which I did try to use, but eventually I left it behind in a hotel bathroom somewhere. Now I just buy cheap stuff. It doesn't seem to make much difference, and I use it so rarely.

01:36:41   As a Zen priest, I probably shouldn't be using makeup at all. Isn't there a precept against lipstick? If not, shouldn't there be? Surely I should be a bit less attached to my physical appearance by now, no? Is my lingering attachment a barometer of my unenlightened state? The author in me is apparently still vain. She is still trying. Is there a time when a woman is officially old enough to stop caring?

PUBLIC FACE

I was forty-one when my first author photos were taken. My publishing house, Viking, asked Marion Ettlinger to photograph me, which was lucky but also quite intimidating, because Marion has shot some of the most iconic author photos of all time, portraits of literary luminaries like Truman Capote, Raymond Carver, and Alice Munro. I remember arriving at her studio and being terribly nervous as I looked through her portfolio and waited for her to set up her reflectors, but she was very kind and very professional. She had a platter of fruit and snacks prepared. She opened a bottle of chilled white wine and poured me a glass. It was all very casual, and we chatted for a while, and eventually she started shooting, and I drank more wine, and by the time we'd finished, I was very relaxed, so when she asked if she could take some extra shots for her private collection, of course I agreed. She rummaged through her costumes and pulled out a faux Persian lamb stole, which she had me wrap around my naked shoulders. She climbed up on a ladder and shot me from above. It was fun. We were goofing around.

Later, when I saw the proofs from the shoot, I was stunned. And I was flattered. I barely recognized myself. Some of the photos were beautiful. Some were scary. Some were cute. Some were prissy. Some were sexy. Overall they were lovely, although I didn't think they looked like me. Oliver agreed, and I could tell he didn't really like them. He thought they were very nice portraits of someone else.

I didn't mind the photo that was chosen for the back flap of *My Year of Meats*. It was coy and cute, and although it made me look a lot younger than my forty-one years, I liked it. I didn't mind being that person for a while. And I didn't mind, six years later, when Marion used the sultry Persian lamb photo in her collection, *Author Photo: Portraits, 1983–2002*. But when my publisher wanted to use that same sultry photo for the publication of my second novel, *All Over Creation*, I balked.

No one could quite understand why, but I had my reasons. For one thing, *All Over Creation* was a novel about potato farming. Gumboots and overalls was more the look I had in mind, not semi-naked-Asian-sex-kitten-wrapped-in-Persian-lamb. But my primary objections were more complex. The photo, while beautiful and sexy, was another projection, and while I didn't mind that in the context of Marion's book, which was all about her gaze and her projections, I didn't feel it should be used to represent me or my work.

And there was another reason, too. The photo had been taken six years earlier, and in those six years, I'd aged. During those years as an author, I'd become aware of public image. I was aware of how harshly women are judged when they show up for readings and events looking like normal people and nothing like their author photos. When I was younger, I'd been guilty of making judgments like this, too, smugly assuming that older women who deliberately chose young-looking publicity photographs must be blind, delusional, or incurably vain. Now that I was aging, I realized how unfair and wrong I'd been. For most women, once we're past a certain age, the changes to our faces are so rapid and radical that it's impossible to keep up, and anyway, who wants to? Who can be bothered? Any serious writer is *writing*, not having her author photo retaken every six months.

It's only now, more than a decade later, that I'm able to understand and articulate my objections to that photograph, and in publishing, you have to pick your battles. In the end, I gave my consent, and the sultry Persian lamb photograph was used to promote the book, although mercifully it was not used on the cover. A very young editorial assistant was the one who finally convinced me by pointing out, respectfully, that at some point in the not-so-distant future, I would probably feel grateful and happy to have such a nice, young-looking picture of myself on record.

She was right, although I feel more bemused and chastened than grateful or happy. Now when

some enthusiastic grad student or festival vol-
unteer meets me at the airport and blurts, *Wow,
you don't look anything like your photo!*, I just smile
and take it as payback for all the times I've judged
others harshly.

TIME CODE 01:39:03

01:39:03   Okay, enough. Focus for a while on what you like about your face, noticing, too, that you have started addressing yourself in the second person, which seems to indicate that you are now a different person from yourself. Hm. Gee. I wonder why would that be?

01:42:33   I like my cheekbones. We have already ascertained this.

01:43:57   I like my hair, the way it's turning silver. I used to dye my hair when I didn't have to, but then I stopped when the roots got too conspicuous.

It was too hard to keep up with, and I couldn't be bothered.

01:45:11   Now I am pinching the skin just below my ears, and I can see how a little facelift would make me look years younger. Just the tiniest little tuck to tighten the loose skin and make my jowls disappear. Wow. Tempting! Jowls are scary! But I know I'll never have surgery. I'm too cowardly. I feel faint during blood tests, or even just getting a shot.

01:47:26   But it's not just because I'm a coward. This is a choice and a very personal one. I've never seriously considered cosmetic surgery, but I've talked about it with women friends, and I know it's a loaded issue, and one that stirs up strong feelings. And because it's a loaded issue, it's hard not to sound apologetic or ruefully defiant if you happen to be considering surgery, and judgmental or dismissively defiant if you're not.

We place such crazy importance on physical appearance in our image-obsessed culture, on youth and beauty to define our sense of self-worth, that aging, by default, becomes a kind of defect, something secret and corrosive and shameful. But to choose to "correct" that defect through surgical means is not a value-neutral solution, either. We still view surgery as a deception or a cheat—cheating time, fooling yourself, deceiving others—so you can't win.* Of course, over time, if surgery becomes the norm, the

---

* Witness the recent online shaming of Renée Zellweger and more recently Uma Thurman, two women actors accused of surgically altering their faces. Where does all that gleeful tabloid umbrage and contempt come from? An actor's face is a mask, a screen for our cultural projections; it both is and isn't her own. So when we suspect an actor of having had plastic surgery, we denounce her not only for trying to deceive us but also for tampering with a face that has become partly ours.

stigma attached to it may lessen, but I don't think it will disappear as long as the aging face, itself, is seen as a problem to be corrected.

What hasn't changed, what seems permanently embedded in our cultural image bank, is the stereotype of aging women, which serves as a kind of barometer for our attitudes. The vanity of the aging queen. The clownish old lady who draws on her eyebrows with a pencil. The celebrity with too much plastic surgery. These ageist images abound, and they are heartbreaking and corrosive.

Nowadays cosmetic surgery is readily available, and people can choose to have a facelift if they can afford it and it makes them happier. I don't have a problem with this. It's just that for me, I don't think it would make me happier. Aside from the fact that I'm a coward, and distressed by the way our culture demeans aging and profits from people's resultant insecurities, I honestly think surgery would make me unhappier. I think it would open up a door to nagging discontent that would be impossible to shut again, and there are other things I'd rather spend my limited time on earth worrying about.

In any case, I've made my choice. I like my gray hair, and surgery is not right for me. I want to look my age. I want to find some beauty in this face, the way it is. I want to be okay with who I am. Right now. Just this.

ORDINATION

When I was ordained as a Soto Zen priest in 2010, I shaved my head as part of the ceremony. The ordination was scheduled to take place at the end of a week-long retreat, and I was excited and nervous. Head-shaving is a symbolic act of renunciation and cutting one's ties with the secular world. The act felt extreme, definitive and transformative, and I'd been looking forward to it. But as the day drew near, I noticed some feelings of resistance creeping in. During the long days of meditation leading up to the ceremony, doubts and questions started to arise, and before I knew it, my mind was churning up little arguments about why head-shaving was anachronistic, sexist, and even inappropriate in present-day America. As Soto Zen practitioners, we'd appropriated this ritual, along with other ceremonial Zen forms, from Japan, but wasn't that just another example of Oriental exoticism? Surely the ritual of head-shaving is maladapted to our western cultural context where, historically, it has meant something very different. In the past, shaving a woman's head was a form of public shaming. It was a punishment for sexual transgression. Lunatics, prisoners, and paupers had shaved heads. And in the present, a woman's loss of hair signifies only one thing: cancer. Is it fair to walk around with a voluntarily shorn head when cancer patients undergoing the ordeal of chemotherapy have no choice? And then there's the gender issue, too. Men shaving their heads is fine, even fashionable.

Men are less attached to their hair—or their hair is less attached to them—but for a woman, hair is part of her identity and central to who she feels she is...

After a couple of hours of this, I'd had enough. During a break between meditation periods, I found a pair of scissors, the electric clippers, and an extension cord, and asked two of my friends to help. We set up in a secluded spot under a tree, behind the lunchroom and overlooking the bay. My hair was longish at the time, reaching my shoulders. I took a thick hank of it from the front and lopped it off with the scissors, and then asked my friends to do the rest. I remember sitting there, watching the herons flying back and forth from the rookery to the tidal flats where they fed, and feeling the sensation of air, and a lightness, too, like a weight was being lifted. They buzzed my head with the electric clippers, and then we cleaned up and I went inside to shower off. I remember feeling excited as I approached the mirror, and feeling some trepidation as well, but when I caught sight of my reflection and saw my skull for the very first time, I felt a powerful sense of recognition.

"There you are!" I whispered. "Where have you been all this time?"

It was like my face had opened up. There was no place to hide, but there was no need to hide, either, and this was a powerful feeling. Hair had become extraneous. In the shower, I didn't need shampoo and conditioner, because there was no longer any separation between my face and my head, or between my head and the rest of my body. I was unified, all one; it was a profound kind of liberation. I toweled off and dressed and went and stood outside. I felt strong and lean, and taller, too, somehow. Cool, ephemeral breezes tickled my skin, and the sun warmed my scalp. It was such a sweet feeling. Such a relief.

TIME CODE 02:00:07

02:00:07 Whew. Made it past hour two. Deep breath. Keep going. Nose. I don't mind my nose. It's my mother's nose, my grandfather's nose, a very fine nose, symmetrical, and when I turn my head, I see it has quite a nice shape in profile. The skin is reddened because I have a cold, but I can flare my nostrils quite splendidly.

Noses are so bizarre! This motile lump of flesh in the middle of the face. They grow bigger as we age, hence the witch's nose. They tingle and run when we get aroused. Funny image, a running nose. Where does it think it's going?

02:05:39   What's the name of that fetching little furrow between nose and upper lip? The one bordered by the two parallel columns that connect the nostrils to the lip peaks? I think it's called the philtren, or philtrum, or something completely unsexy like that. I looked it up once, but now I can't remember. It's such a winsome feature, especially on cats, but what's its function? What's the point? It must do something. Is it some kind of conduit or holding trough? Does it funnel scent more effectively to the nostrils? And if it has no function, why is it there?

Oh, wait, I think I remember. It has something to do with channeling moisture from the mouth to help keep the nose wet, which enhances the sense of smell. I guess it must be vestigial in humans, since we don't need wet noses, but our faces would not be as charming without them.

02:14:14   Mouth. Let's do mouth now. We've talked about the lip peaks, but the proper anatomical name for that part of the upper lip is the "Cupid's bow." I looked that up once, too. My Cupid's bow is still there, valiantly trying to hold the rest of my mouth in place, but my lower lip has pretty much decided to withdraw from the world, and I have to say I resent it. In fact, I've recently developed quite an aversion to my lower lip. I dislike how thin and stingy it's become. I dislike the way it slips between my teeth and disappears, pulling my mouth down at the corners. It makes me look sour and ill-tempered, even when, on the inside, I may be feeling quite content. So I'm really quite annoyed with my lower lip. Why does it insist on misrepresenting me? What is it thinking?

02:22:49   My mom's mouth was crooked. She had a wry and crooked smile, which I've inherited from her. I always loved her smile, and now it makes me smile to see her smile in mine.

HUMOR

My mother had a dry and ironic sense of humor, and it was often hard to know when she was joking. This was particularly true toward the end of her life when she had less to joke about. She had Alzheimer's, but managed to be funny in spite of it.

When we were out and passed a mirror in a shop or restaurant or doctor's office, she'd stop and stare, and then she'd ask me, "Who is that old woman?"

The first time she did this, I immediately assumed she was having an Alzheimer's moment, and so I took a deep breath, swallowed my panic, and explained as gently and reassuringly as I could:

"That's you, Mom."

"No!" she said, shaking her head. "I've never seen that woman before in my life." She frowned at her reflection, and then our eyes met in the mirror, and I realized that this was not the dementia talking. She knew perfectly well that she was looking at herself in the mirror, and she couldn't recognize herself. Both were true. I can relate to this now, and it's only going to get truer as time wears on.

Once she asked me, "How old am I?"

I told her, "You're ninety, Mom."

Her eyes widened. "I am! That's unbelievable! How can I be ninety? I don't feel ninety."

"How old do you feel?"

"Forty."

Deadpan. Perfectly serious.

I laughed. "You can't be forty, Mom. Even I'm older than forty." Actually, I was closer to fifty at the time.

"You are?" she exclaimed. "That's *terrible*!"

"Gee, thanks."

She shook her head. "You know, I must be getting old. I just can't remember anything anymore." She looked up at me and blinked. "How old am I?"

Later on, I asked her, "How does it feel?"

"What?"

"When you can't remember things. Does it frighten you? Do you feel sad?"

"Well, not really. I have this condition, you see. It's called osteo... ost..."

"You mean Alzheimer's?" I said, helping her out.

She looked astonished. "Yes! How on earth did you know that?"

"Just a guess..."

"I can never remember the name," she explained.

"Of course not."

"It affects my memory..."

"...And that's why you can't remember."

She frowned and shook her head. "Remember what?"

"There's not a single thing I can do about it," she told me, when I reminded her. "If there was something I could do and I wasn't doing it, then I could feel sad or depressed. But as it is..." She shrugged.

"So you're okay with it?"

She looked at me, patiently. "I don't have much choice," she explained, "so I may as well be happy."

TIME CODE 02:25:17

02:25:17 It seems I've developed an odd new habit of not closing my mouth completely. I'm having trouble breathing through my nose on account of this cold, so perhaps that's why. I hope that's all it is. I hope this habit corrects itself, because the slack-jawed look is not attractive. It looks imbecilic and reminds me of death. When my father and mother were dying, their jaws went slack and their mouths hung open. A firm jaw is vital. A firm jaw says something about the will to live. A slack jaw says something else.

DEATHBED

I sat with both my parents as they died. I listened to them breathe and watched their faces change, day by day, hour by hour, as life leaked out of them. Their color ebbed, and their cheeks grew hollow. Their jaw muscles slackened, and their mouths hung open. Their skin grew pale and heavy, like wax, melting over their bones.

They looked so different in life—my father, a tall, blond, blue-eyed Caucasian, and my mother a small, brown-eyed, black-haired Asian—but old age and death erased so many of the differences between them, and in the end, they looked surprisingly similar.

My parents had me late, when they were in their early forties; they were already sixty when I turned eighteen. I never knew them when they had young faces. To me, they were always old and aging, and so when I was young, it was impossible for me to recognize resemblances or see their young faces in mine. My mother always insisted that I took after my father. *Two peas in a pod*, she used to say, and I took her word for it. When I was little, this made me fiercely proud.

Now, at fifty-nine, I'm finally catching up with them. Now I'm at the age they were when I remember them best, and even though they are both dead, they will be with me for the rest of my life—in my aging eyes, my aging nose, my aging mouth, my aging cheekbones, just below the surface of my aging skin. They will be with me when I die, too, and I find this reassuring. As I sat by my mother's side and held her hand and watched her, I remember thinking, *I'm going to do this, too, some day. This is what dying looks like. This is what Dad looked like when he died, and what I'm going to look like, too. Like Mom and Dad.* It was comforting to know what I would look like. It made death a little less frightening, a little more intimate, a little more dear.

TIME CODE 02:31:11

02:31:11   Just under half an hour left. What did I hope to accomplish in these three hours? Did I expect to gain some insight? To come to some greater understanding and acceptance of who I am? To develop some Zen-like detachment?

FACE-TO-FACE

When Dōgen Zenji was twenty-three years old, he boarded a ship from Japan to China on a quest for enlightenment. In China, he traveled around, visiting many monasteries, until finally, in 1225, he found his true teacher, Rujing. He wrote about this first meeting in an essay called *Face-to-Face Transmission*, or *Menju* in Japanese:

> I first offered incense and bowed formally to Rujing in the abbot's room—Wondrous Light Terrace—on the first day, the fifth month, of the first year of the Baoqing Era of Great Song. He also saw me for the

first time. Upon this occasion he transmitted dharma to me, finger to finger, face to face, and said, "The dharma gate of face-to-face transmission from buddha to buddha, ancestor to ancestor, is actualized now."*

I imagine a sparking blue arc of electricity, like a lightning bolt, traveling from Rujing to Dōgen as he transmits the true dharma eye. Face-to-face transmission is an essential part of Zen and the Zen lineage. It points to an understanding that can't be taken from books and can't be conveyed through words. It's an understanding that can only emerge in the intimacy of the face-to-face meeting between student and teacher, and it's been passed down this way since the time of the Buddha.

---

* Eihei Dōgen, *Treasury of the True Dharma Eye*, trans. Kazuaki Tanahashi (Boston & London: Shambhala Publications, 2012), 569–70.

In their meetings, Rujing taught Dōgen the practice of *shikantaza*, or "just sitting," a simple objectless style of Zen meditation. Through this practice, one day, Dōgen experienced a breakthrough or awakening, which he called the "dropping off of body and mind." Later, he would describe this in his first written meditation instructions:

Hence, you should stop searching for phrases and chasing after words. Take the backward step and turn the light inward. Your body-mind of itself will drop off and your original face will appear. If you want to attain just this,* immediately practice just this.†

---

* "Just this" is a phrase that is central to Zen teachings and often translated as "suchness."

† Eihei Dōgen, *Fukanzazengi* [Universal Instructions for Zazen] in *Treasury of the True Dharma Eye*, 907.

This experience of meeting his original face was a turning point for Dōgen. He spent four years practicing and studying with Rujing and then returned to Japan. Upon his return, someone asked him what he had learned in China.

"I have come back empty-handed," Dōgen answered. "What I know is this: that my eyes are horizontal and my nose is vertical. I can no longer be misled."

TIME CODE 02:38:41

02:38:41 Three hours have gone by quickly. Have my feelings about my face changed? Hard to say. But some of the severity seems to have drained from my features. My face looks more familiar, softer, and less judgmental, and so I feel a bit fonder of it now. The tension under my skin seems to have relaxed and my eyes are less wary and sad. They look clear, and my face looks nicer to me now than it did at the beginning. Is this some kind of progress?

2:53:01 And now I think it's sweet the way my finger wants to reach to touch the blemish on my chin. The skin is chapped there and rough to the touch, but my finger knows it's healing. After so many years, my fingertips know these surfaces so well, and it's nice of them to take such good care of me. And it's nice of my eyes to forgive themselves and to forgive the rest of my face, too.

2:56:57 ...58... 59... and counting... It's a beautiful spring day, and the cherry tree outside my window is in bloom, and as soon as I'm done, I'm going outside. I'm going to get a latte and a lemon bar and sit on a bench in Tompkins Square Park and watch the squirrels and the dogs and the pigeons and all the pretty people...

2:58:36 And maybe here's a bit of insight: My face is and isn't me. It's a nice face. It has lots of people in it. My parents, my grandparents, and their grandparents, all the way back through time

and countless generations to my earliest ancestors—all those iterations are here in my face,
along with all the people who've ever looked at
me. And the light and shadows are here, too, the
joys, anxieties, griefs, vanities, and laughter. The
sun, the rain, the wind, the broom poles, and the
iron fences that have distressed my face with lines
and scars and creases—all here.

2:59:23 Say hi to your face, face. Say hi to the
world.

2:59:42 Good. Now close your mouth. Go ahead
and raise your eyebrow. Roll your eyes a little,
and smile, and...

3:00:00 ...that's it! We're done!

MISE EN ABYME

The mirror room (鏡の間, pronounced *kagami-no-ma*) is the inner sanctum of a Noh theater, located between the dressing room and the curtain through which the actor makes his entrance onto stage. The word 間 (*ma*) in Japanese can refer either to a physical location, like a room, or to an interval or moment in time. In this liminal space then, the actor, dressed in an elaborate brocade costume, pauses to collect himself in silence. He sits in front of a full-length mirror and focuses his mind and attention, and then with great care, he picks up his mask. Holding it reverently in his hands, he brings it to his face, and for a moment the actor and the mask gaze at each other. "This is the moment," Udaka writes, "when he pours all his emotions into the mask, and simultaneously, a sacred interlude in which the role he is about to play fills him."*

The actor bows to the mask, turns it, and, with the help of an assistant, positions it on his face.

> In that instant, he is transformed into the protagonist of the story. Thus the *kagami-no-ma* functions as a ritual space where the magical powers of the Noh mask are instilled in the actor.†

Although lacking the brocade and elements of ancient sacred ritual, a novel can be a kind of

---

* Udaka, *The Secrets of Noh Masks*, 127.

† Udaka, *The Secrets of Noh Masks*, 153–54.

mirror room, too. It, too, is a liminal space, silent, bound by certain rituals and full of magic. The writer enters and seats herself in front of her reflection in the mirror. She collects herself and focuses her attention, and then she picks up a mask. She gazes at it and positions it on her face, and at that moment she is transformed into the protagonist of her story, looking out through its eyes at her reflection in the mirror, made strange by the face of another. It's a complex sensation, impossible to describe exactly, but, oh, such lingering sweetness!

Then, because the world of novels is an endless hall of mirrors, that moment of transformation of writer into character is echoed by the reader when he or she opens the book and enters the mirror room, dons the mask, and becomes the character, too. This is why we read novels, after all, to see our reflections transformed, to enter another's subjectivity, to wear another's face, to live inside another's skin.

My observation experiment has been a kind of kagami-no-ma, too. Although very different from the objectless shikantaza meditation that Dōgen taught, the meditative investigation of my face in the mirror reminds me of another essay of his, in which he wrote, "To study the buddha way is to study the self. To study the self is to forget the self. To forget the self is to be actualized by the myriad things (of the world)."* The observation experiment, like meditation, has had the effect of waking me up to things that I ordinarily would not notice or would have ignored. In the days

---

* Eihei Dōgen, *Genjō Kōan*, in *Treasury of the True Dharma Eye*, trans. Kazuaki Tanahashi (Boston & London: Shambhala Publications, 2012), 30.

and weeks and months that have followed, I find myself looking at people's faces more closely. There's a new subjectivity in my gaze when I look at others. Their faces mirror mine, and my face mirrors theirs, and this gives rise to a feeling of recursive kindliness and kinship that I haven't felt in quite this way before. It's unlikely that the people I pass on the street have ever spent three hours staring at their faces in the mirror—who would, after all?—but I imagine that they, too, have intimate, if unarticulated, relationships with their reflected faces that are as complex and fraught as mine. Their faces, like all faces, are time batteries, and maybe even works of art.

So now, on the subway, while the other passengers are enthralled by their devices, I take the opportunity to observe them, unseen. What would it feel like to look like that woman? Who does she see in her face in the mirror? Do her jowls bother her, or is she more preoccupied by the lines on her forehead? Does she have a mirror face? A mask? What grief carved that deep groove between her eyebrows? What does that man think when he shaves every morning? Does it worry him that he looks more like his father every day? What rituals does he perform? Does he talk to himself? What does he say? Does he suck in his gut, and inspect his nostrils for hairs? Does he thrust out his chin and turn his head from side to side, trying to catch a glimpse of his profile? Who broke his nose?

Maybe this is just more solipsistic projection, but we all spend a lot of time alone with our reflections, and here, in the kagami-no-ma, is where we are most naked and most vulnerable to our own self-love and self-loathing. The mirror room is where, every day, we confront our hopes and desires, our delusions and disappointments, our aging and our mortality, and there's something sweet and sad and incredibly brave about our willingness to do so. We put on our makeup and our mirror faces. We suck in our cheeks, and lift our chins, and turn our heads to better deflect the light and shadows. We greet our mothers and fathers with affection or dismay. We engage in subterfuge and wishful thinking, but we keep coming back, every morning, and look ourselves in the eye and somehow pull ourselves together enough to get out the door and face another day. This, in itself, is kind of heroic.

But let's not get carried away. Let's not be misled. Because, after all is said and done, all we really know is this: our eyes are horizontal and our noses are vertical. Just this.

ABOUT THE AUTHOR

RUTH OZEKI is a novelist, filmmaker, and Zen Buddhist priest. Her first two novels, *My Year of Meats* (1998) and *All Over Creation* (2003), have been translated into eleven languages and published in fourteen countries. Her most recent work, *A Tale for the Time Being* (2013), won the *LA Times* Book Prize, was shortlisted for the Man Booker Prize and National Book Critic's Circle Award, and has been published in over thirty countries. Ruth's documentary and dramatic independent films, including *Halving the Bones*, have been shown on PBS, at the Sundance Film Festival, and at colleges and universities across the country.

A longtime Buddhist practitioner, Ruth was ordained as a priest in 2010 and is affiliated with the Brooklyn Zen Center and the Everyday Zen Foundation. She lives in British Columbia and New York City, and is currently the Elizabeth Drew Professor of Creative Writing at Smith College.